Some Days: Poetry of a Psychotherapist

Linda Leedy Schneider

Plain View Press
P.O. 42255
Austin, TX 78704

plainviewpress.net
pk@plainviewpress.net
512-441-2452

Copyright © 2011 Linda Leedy Schneider All rights reserved under International and Pan-American Copyright Conventions. No part of this book may be reproduced or distributed in any form or by any means, or stored in a data base or retrieval system, without written permission from the author. All rights, including electronic, are reserved by the author and publisher.

ISBN: 978-1-935514-08-4
Library of Congress Control Number: 2011930966

Cover photo from Irochka@Dreamstime®.com
Cover design by Sherry L. Pilisko

Acknowledgements

Grateful acknowledgements to the following publications, in which these poems first appeared, often in different versions: *Clockwise Cat:* "The Bird and the Cymbals;" *Glass:* "Conversation: Emergency Room;" *JAW Magazine:* "I Am Always Forgetting Something;" *Leaf Garden:* "Marché, Paris;" *Midwest Poetry Review:* "Widow in Spring;" *Midwest Literary Magazine:* "Birthday;" *Miranda Literary Magazine*: "Iraqi Woman Attends a Wedding," "Look, Mama I Am Writing a Poem," "Perfect Pruning Shears;" *Poets Against War:* "War Games;" *Pudding Magazine: The International Journal of Applied Poetry:* "After Working in An Albanian Orphanage," "First Day Volunteering in an Albania Orphanage," "Tirana, Albania;" *Pulsar, UK:* Sunset-February, 2003;" *Rattle:* "I Reclaim," "She Had Always Been Able;" *SNReview:* "To a Poem Written Yesterday;" *The Ambassador Poetry Project:* "Concentric Rings," "The Monarch Are in the Milkweed," "People Are Disappearing in Michigan;" *The Heartland Review*: "The Day After a Lunar Eclipse;" *The Pedestal Magazine:* "Albania: Day 14," "My Hands Speak After Thirty-Five Years," "Oak Leaves;" *The Sow's Ear:* "Conversation: Alzheimer's Unit;" *The Spoon River Poetry Review:* "Tomato;" *Word Riot:* "Five Minutes Between Therapy Clients," "Wind, Water, Fire, and Stone;" *Not a Muse, The Inner Lives of Women: A World Poetry Anthology* (Haven Books 2009); "Before the Telephone Rang," "Letter to My Long-Term Husband."

Some of these poems have also been included in: *Through the Lattice: Poetry of a Psychotherapist* (Argonne House Press 2002), and *Through My Window: Poetry of a Psychotherapist* (Pudding House Publications 2007).

*To my Husband
and our Family*

*And the day came when the risk
to remain tight in a bud was more painful
than the risk it took to blossom*
—Anaïs Nin

*Only those who will risk going too far
can possibly find out how far one can go*
—T.S. Eliot

Contents

I. There Is Something She Wants To Say   13

    Five Minutes Between Therapy Clients   15
    Albania: Day Fourteen   16
    Words Struggle in Me   17
    Oak Leaves   18
    My Hands Speak After 35 Years   19
    Wind, Water, Fire, and Stone   20
    There Is Something She Wants To Say   21
    First Day Volunteering in Albania   23
    Albanian Orphan   24
    Orphanage, Tirana, Albania   25
    After Working in an Albanian Orphanage   26
    Sunset–February, 2003   27
    Collateral Damage   28
    War Games   29
    Iraqi Woman Attends a Wedding   30
    Immigration   31
    A Poem for Peace   32

II. She Had Always Been Able   33

    To a Poem Written Yesterday   35
    A Child Awakens   37
    Marché, Paris   38
    The Monarchs Are in the Milkweed   39
    She Had Always Been Able   40
    Concentric Rings   42
    Peony's Lament   44
    The Theft of the Peony   45
    She Is a Green Pepper   46
    Cherry Orchard   47
    Woman's Song   48
    The Bird and the Cymbals   49

III. Sparks in a Blizzard — 51

Morning	53
Keystone	54
Hanging On	55
Sparks in a Blizzard	56
Breakfast	57
Jasmine in the Morning	58
Blue Five Pound Weights	59
Conversations: Emergency Room	60
Some Days	62
I Didn't Think of You	63
The Day After a Lunar Eclipse	65

IV. Cycles — 67

Look, Mama, I'm Writing a Poem	69
I Am Always Forgetting Something	70
Alzheimer's Unit: Room #653	71
She Forgets My Name Again	73
Premature Pulling at the Botanical Gardens	75
First Snow	76
Widow In Spring	77
Bouquet	78
Cycles	79
Psychotherapist's Waiting Room	80
Be Fruitful and Multiply	81
Timing	82
Spider Plant	83

V. I Reclaim   **85**

    Language   87
    Perfect Pruning Shears   88
    Risk of Impalement   90
    Letter to My Long-Term Husband   91
    Before the Telephone Rang   92
    Conversation: Alzheimer's Unit   93
    Rain Washes   95
    Birthday   96
    France After the Affair   97
    People Are Disappearing in Michigan   98
    Tomato   99
    I Reclaim   101

    About the Author   103

I.

There Is Something She Wants To Say

Five Minutes Between Therapy Clients

Through my window I see
swans float on a man-made
pond with a concrete fountain.
Look into an impressionist oil
over my desk. Lush roses
and always the one fallen perfect petal.
No insects, no rain, no rot.

In these minutes I see
the painting's imperfect perfection
for the first time:
after the woman who found
her husband naked with her sister-in-law
and before the college professor
who doesn't know why he cries.

Albania: Day Fourteen

She follows a winding path
from the state orphanage to the Adriatic Sea,
which is clotted with oil on its Eastern shore.
A boy walks by and holds up a fistful
of writhing eels, a Medusa head,

like the eel she ate the night before,
while a blind guitarist played,
and fried eel was offered
followed by fig cake studded with fly legs.
Because the road to Skodra passed over a ravine,
they had walked a rope-hung bridge one
by one to get to that state dinner.

It was a time of war,
gunfire over the mountains in Kosovo,
infants dying for lack of IV tubing,
rickets, ringworm, cleft palates,
    eels, and bodies.

So last night when the music started
and that man said, "Come,"
she did and danced till it all was gone.
Nothing but two bodies and the beat
    —Nothing but bodies.

Words Struggle in Me

    the way babies once kicked,
full of possibility,
but needing time to incubate,
to drink from my body
until time to line up and be born.
I take my words to see Monet and Olendorf,
read them poetry by Oliver and Eliot,
let them inhale fresh bread and damp sheets,
hear Bach and The Beatles.
I carry them to the gym
where they roll around
as I count steps and reps.
I let them consider rhythm.
They travel with me to the grocery store
where I pick up turkey and provolone,
two apples, and dark chocolate.
The words arrange and rearrange
themselves as I collect my groceries.
I take my words on walks,
let them play with other people's words,
even trade some away and take on others
like amoebae exchange parts
for recreation or procreation.
A writer must be ruthless
with her words.
They are only the bricks:
not the breath, the baby, or the poem.

Oak Leaves

I.
I am Alyssum, the last flower alive in this planter.
It's November, for God's sake, and here I am small,
pure like baby's breath or bridal lace.
I bloom among the blighted.

Geranium's flare of fuchsia
is now black and curled into itself
like an infant pulls in his legs
to remember the sea.
Daisy's only eye is closed.
She holds her seeds close.

This is Michigan—ripped by glaciers
and soothed by the subsequent sea.
Great Lakes wash over wounds, mastodon bones,
Petoskey stones. Sleeping Bear Dune keeps watch,
but Lake Michigan steals sand
with every wave and sends back snow
to kill November flowers.

White on white, I will succumb.
November, trees empty except for the oak
that hangs on to its dead,
carries them—brown, broken, afraid to let go.

II.
My left eye hurts, waters, clouds this page.
I have sliced onions to make stock.
Soup—what else can I do when words wither,
and she hangs on brittle, crumpled,
as afraid as the oak leaves?

My Hands Speak After 35 Years

Paris was served on a fresh plate
with honey on the side,
and I took its hand.
My left hand says this is true.

I call my right, the one that thought
we should have married the doctor.
It touches my hair as the phone rings.
Why haven't you called?

my husband of thirty-five years asks.
My right hand cups my right breast,
the one that always tightens first,
the one my husband seems to prefer.

I am 57. I am 57.
Next year I will be 58, whether or not
I accept Paris, which speaks of music,
poetry, and the dance that could save us all.

My right hand remembers my husband.
My baby, my child, he said,
as he held his hand on my belly,
waited for an answer from my womb.

My left hand says, *That child is 33
and now mother to her own children.*
My left hand says, *Your womb is gone.*
My left hand says, *Next year you will be 58,*

*and may never again be offered
Paris   on any plate.*

Wind, Water, Fire, and Stone

It is the stone in my pocket,
the rough one, with its vein of quartz,
a hidden, forever fire. I can touch
that stone, and no one knows.

It is the beat of a bass drum
that calls my body to consider rhythm,
to remember the wash of waves
that carried us forward in the march
through twilight into night.

It is that sunny day in March
that stirs my desire for more,
yet I feel suspended
like a stemmed cherry
captured in a cube of ice.

Everything circles and dances
like tongues of fire on the hearth,
like a willow caught in the wind,
like the confusion of waves before a storm,
like the stone that blazes in my hand.

There Is Something She Wants To Say

She looks west over Lake Michigan,
sees the pink echo of sunrise.
Her mother forgets her name;
she brings her lavender.
Her children's children circle her table.
How can this be? She is twenty- three.

No, she is eight and can finally leave her block.
    She goes to the woods with a man
        who promises wild flowers.

She is twenty and away from that woods.
    She is free and dances to ancient rhythms.
        No one can own her body now.

She is thirty and rocks her first daughter.
    Reads to her. The other child in her belly
        dances, and the pages turn.

She is forty. Gives away her womb;
    orgasm now in minor key. She appears to be
        as free as the girl who left her block,

But, when ancient rhythms call her again,
she smothers her dance.

She is fifty, Sunday dinners, grandchildren. She does
    not tell them about people who offer too much,
        the second chance you can take or smother,
            the ancient dance that ties you to the chair.

It's a sunny day.
Empty vase beside her,
she cradles a bouquet of lavender
 and begins to sway.
She is twenty-three.

First Day Volunteering in Albania

Don't give them anything,
they said.

Airport boy asks
for the gum
from my mouth

A foot reaches through
bars on her cradle,
and she rocks herself

Rats leap
to escape
hospital cats

Pseudo-doctors
deliver more babies
into blue enamel pans.

A child clings to the edge
of my half-open van window
as we pull away.

Albanian Orphan

He lives

in the attic of the orphanage
where the *terribles* are kept.
His clubfoot causes him
to crawl like a crab.

His mother left him
when her milk curdled,
turned to stone in her breasts.
"She visited some,"
they say, "then found work
in a kitchen in Skodra."

He waits

by the cracked west window,
looks to the Adriatic Sea
where bloated fish float
in slicks of oil.

He watches

for his mother
as gulls carry carrion
to their open-mouthed babies.

Orphanage, Tirana, Albania

A child peers through
a broken, barred window.
Rats tumble like acrobats
as we enter.

Water drips from overhead.
*It was the bombs. Watch out
for the holes in the floor.*

We find a room
filled with babies
chanting
their own lullabies.

Cups of gray soup
glaze over with grease
as I hold hunger
to my milkless breasts.

After Working in an Albanian Orphanage

I gaze through my skylight
    see broken windows,

select Mexican tiles
    remember uneven floors,

use hair spray
    think of head lice,

file a nail
    see a withered hand,

put on makeup
    picture ringworm,

eat breakfast
    think of hollow bellies.

I hold my children
    and feel   alone.

Sunset—February, 2003

just before bombing began in Iraq

The leafless trees
on the far shore
of my frozen lake
stand in rows like
soldiers on review.
I remember a music
man, painter of pictures
whose deferment
ran out. He left me
that June with a bouquet
of promises
that finally fell lifeless
from their stems.

Again, the trees
across my lake
cast long dark
shadows
toward the East.

Collateral Damage

for Clara, my grandmother, 1894–1918

A pot of spaghetti sauce simmers;
streams run like veins
down the steamy kitchen window.
Her hands stained gray,
a girl pulls at pieces of yesterday's paper,
shreds the words of war,
tears them to confetti
to bless the peace parade tomorrow.
The war to end all wars is over,
but soldiers will bring back Spanish flu
which will make her mother
now adding pasta to a boiling pot
one of the last casualties of that war.

War Games

The orchard is a white cloud
wanting to be cherries.

Children run round and round its edges
like bees circling blossoms.

Finally they enter the forbidden space,
tear off blossoms, look into their hidden pink centers,
taste nectar, and *dance*,

find a wooden box abuzz with bees,
remember being stung,
pain like a flaming needle.
They have fire.
The orchard needs to be saved.

Wrinkled leaves flare after the matchbook is struck.
Bees hurt. Bees sting. Let's kill them all!
the children chant as blue fire rises carrying flaming bees.

Flying torches,
like flaming children
running from napalm
in Viet Nam.

The bees zigzag, circle, fall.
The orchard is gone   just one match.

Iraqi Woman Attends a Wedding

in response to an article in The New York Times

They drove across the border
to Jordan, rented a room.
She unpacked the black denim dress
large enough to hide a pregnancy
or a suicide belt.
She took a taxi with her husband
to the wedding at the Radisson.

Did he kiss her good-bye
before he *pushed her out*
of that ballroom
as she fumbled with her belt.
Did they lie the night before
like familiar spoons in a drawer,
his arm cradling her breasts,
read newspapers over omelets,
leave their belongings
or pack efficiently and…?

No, No! They planned never
to need anything again.

It must all be there
in that furnished room
the woman ran back to,
the belt packed with fifteen pounds
of explosives and metal ball bearings
to kill as many people as possible,
still strapped around her waist.

Immigration

sentences found in The Grand Rapids Press
Sunday, May 4, 2008

Infant girls
by the thousands are abandoned every year in China.
Don't sneak into America, a country founded
by immigrants and priding itself on opportunity.
We are taking control of our borders.
Terrorist attacks revived immigration debates.
U. S. adoptions have boomed in Viet Nam.
Americans adopted more than 1,200 Vietnamese
children. Adoptions have quadrupled from China.
Estimated Cost: $20,000 to $25,000, 91% Female.

TV footage showed six of those who died
Friday trying to cross into the United States
from Mexico.

To some the fence is a symbol of the Berlin Wall.
The Homeland Security Department counters,
"The plan is already working."

A Poem for Peace

When men hurled harpoons,
devil whales, the great whites,
attacked ships in the Baja.

Females could be taken easily.
These hunters targeted calves first
knowing a great white never leaves her young.

Now whales come up to boats in the Baja,
allow their heads to be touched,
are even thought to *bring their babies*
to the boats to show them off.

II.

She Had Always Been Able

To a Poem Written Yesterday

> *I was working on the proof of one of my poems all morning,*
> *and took out the comma. In the afternoon I put it back in again*
> —Oscar Wilde

You incubated in darkness,
were born in a yellow notebook,
loved like any fantasy child.

Then the rearranging began.
Was one line too long?
      I amputated.
Did you need more color?
      I gave you the fuchsia of peonies,
      the fresh green of new growth.

Then attached the amputation to a short sibling.
Your song began to sound listless.
I added some liquid alliteration.

Your rhythm seems off.
I tapped my fingers,
beat a drum, marched
and again   added
                and subtracted
                          parts,

until you didn't resemble the poem I loved
yesterday...

So now, after seven versions,
singing, amputating, drumming,
and reading into a recorder,

I return to the original pushed out on the page
and find I still love it   unconditionally.
It's uneven edges,
the yellow and fuchsia dance
between green reattached lines.
One line seems to sing to another, a heart beats.
Yesterday's poem has decided to stay.

A Child Awakens

    to the bars of her crib and their shadows,
hears clashing voices from downstairs.
She reaches for the shadows
cast through her ivy-shrouded window,
sees her own hand repeated on the sheet.
She tries to hold a shadow.
Her hand changes everything.
Wind shakes the windows;
soon the ivy shudders in rain.
The girl's canvas has gone blank.
She curls down under her blanket
having learned long ago not to cry.

Marché, Paris

A boy offers bouquets of peony buds
dressed in baby's breath at the market on Wilson.
She sees crepes being cooked on a metal barrel
then blanketed with cheese,
drizzled with only the egg white,
the yolk still captured
in the broken shell.
The white is smoothed over the crepe and cheese
like a fresh bed sheet
and finally the puncture and spreading of the yolk.

"Whole wheat crepes," the man says
as he rolls them to tubes.
She eats at his checkered table,
then gathers prawns, escargot, a quilt of greens,
tomatoes, and fresh goat cheese.

As she leaves, the boy is still asking
each shopper to consider his peonies,
but the shoppers know the buds are small, hard
and tight, too tight like the closed eyes of a kitten
born too soon, or the skin over a bellyful of baby,
or the smile of the boy's mother who hides nearby.

The woman buys one of the boy's bouquets,
cuts the stems back hard,
places them in warm water,
carries the vase to the sun.
One of the buds opens wide, luminous, lacy,
a sphere that makes the woman remember words
like *egg, baby, puncture, quilt, boy, mother.*
She pulls the solitary blossom to her breast
and begins to rock.

The Monarchs Are in the Milkweed

She runs through the geometry
of apple trees to the meadow
where Queen Anne rules,
proud of her purple difference,
daisies bend in the breeze, hold secrets in soft petals,
and matronly milkweed waits. Monarchs circle,
swirl in orange masses like flames on a hearth.
The girl drops her net, holster, black boots,
and floats around the milkweed with the butterflies.
Her arms flutter.
Finally she sits still as a Petoskey stone,
holding hexagonal memories of the ancient sea,
curls into herself, watches the harlequin dance,
breaks a thick leathery leaf, touches it to her lips.
A monarch lands on her hand tastes the milk. She
sees the spotted body, black legs ending in claws;
orange dust flies around the pumping wings.
She lies back on the soft grass, watches
the butterfly walk across her belly, then soar
to the highest apple tree.
She gathers Queen Anne's lace and daisies.
The empty net slung over her shoulder
bumps her bare legs
where orange dust clings like a memory.

She Had Always Been Able

    to fall down deep into a flower.
The wallpaper of the front hall
that held the phone
swirled with cabbage roses.
She counted leaves and petals
as she listened to neighbors talk
of gardeners, the new minister,
and one wandering husband.
Peonies swirled as she heard,
Now it's the teacher, Miss Rose
that he is seeing.

The first grade classroom
with its lighted aquarium,
gliding guppies, clean blackboards,
stacks of papers ordered by color
had been safe.
She didn't need to count leaves,
petals, or panes of glass
to settle her mind
until she strayed and listened in
on that phone call.

Mr. Clay with Miss Rose,
the thought made
the green walls pulse in and out.
She began to count chalk,
papers on the bulletin board.
Mr. Clay had three children.
Mrs. Clay, they said, *was crying.*
She counted and recounted
her fingers and toes.

She stepped over every crack
on her way home worrying
her mother had died
or left with the postman.
She washed her hands
five times in the empty house
before going to the swirling roses
to pick up that black phone
again.

Concentric Rings

written after seeing AfterGlow, a photograph, from Junkyard Rhapsody by Eugene Bradford

These could be wedding rings
cast off or placed on a bedside table,
perhaps bought on a day in April
when the pink magnolia tree showered
its one-day blessing like confetti,
and the man and the woman expected
showers of pink petals forever.
A day when he touched
the hair that cascaded down her back
like it was Rumpelstiltskin's gold,
and she knew he would shelter her
and the child soon to move in her belly.
She pictured him placing this ring on her finger
in her white steepled church
on the shore of Lake Michigan.
But on that day in June,
the Lake vomited decaying alewives.
Waves bit at the shore, carried sand away
with each invasion. The foghorn moaned
through the night and that day.
A black helicopter moved back and forth
along the shoreline from the Saugatuck sand dunes
to the iron and concrete Grand Haven pier.
Waves washed over the top of the red lighthouse.
Thunder filled the church, and the lights failed.

The baby in her belly moved
as the man placed the ring on her finger.
Petals were pounded
from the apple and cherry trees.
I am the child who demanded
to be born, and their rings rusted
like the rings in AfterGlow.

Peony's Lament

We are praised
for our passing pinkness,
layer on layer of lace,
blooms as big as baby bonnets,
but beauty is often heavy.
Some of us sag to the soil,
brown at our edges,
fold inward,
and collapse
like tired dancers
in wrinkled dresses.

The Theft of the Peony

When I was five…

I.
I would not have taken
the marigolds with their yellow
fringed faces.
I let them all keep
their trumpeting daffodils,
zinnias with petals layered
like pheasant feathers,
snapdragons balanced
on each other's heads.
I didn't take the green gazing ball
or the roses trained to a trellis,
but when those peony buds
spilled white petals
lacy like a wedding dress,
and one sagged.
I took it and
carried the stolen blossom
to my bedroom.

II.
Later, when I opened
my drawer to admire
the flower alone. I found
the peony wet and crumpled
like a used tissue
and a permanent brown stain
on my pink nightgown.

She Is a Green Pepper

A globe of goodness.
She rests on her haunches,
wears her favorite hat.

She blushes red,
wishes to be wanted
for her soft flesh.

She longs to strip for you—
run in scalloped circles.

Heavy with seed,
she just waits
for the cut
of your knife.

Cherry Orchard

A checkerboard of trees
holds blossoms virginal white,
waits for the bees to start
the seeds in these ovaries,
form the hard stone left
after the flesh is eaten.

It happened in a
red convertible;
all she thought good
fell to the floor
with her pink skirt.

Later she would remember
and even confess
as she sucked the wafer,
swallowed the wine,
but she had been touched.
She would bloom.

Woman's Song

Mother touches and tends,
sings her a song of the moon.
Father throws her into the air
just for the reward of her laughter.
Mother looks to the moon's half face,
welcomes its tide, its blood.
Father builds towers
for the girl to topple, over and over again.
Father fears the moon, the changing tides,
and the blood that will come to his daughter.
The girl plays with blocks and babies.
Her breasts tingle. Trees reach
for her as she passes in the night.
This moon-ridden girl turns in
on herself and out toward the world.
She waves once
to her father and mother
who stand on the doorstep.

The Bird and the Cymbals

an ekphrastic response to music

Caught in the pulse of the percussion
somewhere between the bells and the cymbals
is a silver bird with a single note
that pleads, *Hear me. Listen to my song.*
This sky-flyer is held by a repeating beating cycle.
The music calls the winged one,
but leaves her afraid.

Here comes the shimmering shower of the cymbal.
Percussion man, are you playing with this silver bird?
She wants to look again into your cymbals, find
the source of the sound that reminds her of the sea.
She needs to see who she is—who she was
    before this song seduced her.

As the music rises to crescendo,
the silver bird spreads her wings wide
beats empty air
then refolds her wings and settles
tries to become a peaceful
    one-note bird again.

III.

Sparks in a Blizzard

Morning

Last night's load
cools in the dishwasher.
Cups with brown stains
wait in line.

A tulip opens and drops
her yellow sex on my counter.
I cross my legs
and write poetry.

Keystone

> *on viewing an Andrew Goldsworthy arch at Meijer Gardens,*
> *Grand Rapids Michigan*

Pink and gray Scottish granite
ascends from a polished maple floor
each slab balanced separately—
no glue, no artificial connection.
Two columns carry their own weight
then reach toward each other,
find the keystone, completion, an arch,
like a man and a woman coming together,

like love,
    sturdy as stone,
        fragile as each connection.

Hanging On

The *Yellow Pages* are open to M—*massage*.
A blue pot of chives languishes next to the book.
Since September when she brought the pot inside,
half of the hollow leaves have died.
Chives are not like Swedish ivy, ivy so compliant
that she can pluck the hand-like leaves
and use them as molds for melted chocolate.
Sometimes red liquid leaks from the leaves
as she separates them from the plant,
but she brushes it aside and garnishes
dessert plates with perfect chocolate leaves.
Chives are not like the ficus tree
that drops leaves at every breeze,
not sturdy like the spider plant
that carries its offspring on strings.
These chives are not ready to be clipped
for stew or stirred into cream cheese.
The chives in her blue ceramic pot
may not see spring again.
She carefully separates
the dead from the living
whenever she brings water.

Sparks in a Blizzard

A silver plow scatters sparks
beneath her bedroom window
as it scrapes to bare pavement.
Blizzard in the mitten state.

She remembers the fairy tale
about a girl sent to the streets
in a snowstorm to sell matches.
The girl used them, one
by one, to warm herself
and was found
frozen in the morning.

She, too, is running
out of ways to warm herself.
There is coffee in a thick blue mug,
and a man sings
in the next room, but
she wants a blaze
in this blizzard.

Breakfast

Be careful of an ending that seems only satisfactory
—Steven Dunn

They are each in a bubble.
She no longer pierces hers
to reach him.
She wants to ride the
carousel in Avignon,
dance again
with the man in black.
She remembers a man
who played flamenco guitar,
poured white wine into iced glasses,
used his fingers in ways
that made her sing.

Jasmine in the Morning

A heron perches on a piling,
supervises the sunrise.
Sun splashes pink stripes
into the morning sky.
Last night's jasmine
sends sensual signals
through my room.
I remember Kresge's:
jasmine perfume
in a golden bottle,
two girls squeezed
into a photo booth
after trying on daring dresses,
broad-brimmed hats,
even bras they would never buy,
like they tried on sophomore boys
they would never wed.

Blue Five Pound Weights

    rest one on the other
like relaxed lovers.
I lifted these weights
while my daughters floated in my womb,
after sleeping on the floor
of my father's hospital room,
before telling my mother she must dress
and come to a new home,
while my daughter timed
the contractions of a premature labor,
after the baby was born too early.
I lift these blue weights when
I am considering leaving again.
These weights are thirty-one years old.
Sometimes, I don't touch them for months.

Conversations: Emergency Room

Where does it hurt?
I have a pain in my chest that goes up into my left jaw.
I have never felt a pain like this before.
Where does it hurt?
To the ends of each hair, through my bones,
the space that held my uterus, but mostly in my heart.

What medications do you take?
Cenestin, a natural hormone replacement,
trazadone for sleep.
What medications do you take?
I drank mother's milk.
I take in my husband's sperm.

Does that hurt?
My veins are hard to find.
They are small, and they roll.
Does that hurt?
Yes, like fire, empty eyes, my mother's tears.
I have perfected being hard to find
and rolling from pain.
In fact, I am such an expert,
I try to teach others.

We'll just put this on your chest.
We'll need a running EKG.
Are you OK?
Yes.
Are you OK?
As OK as I can be with
seven plastic circles pasted
over and around my breast.
The right breast, always the better of the two,
still holds the heat of a strange man's hand.

Is your blood pressure always this high?
What is it?
Is your blood pressure always this high?
No, I am afraid.
I am in the wallpaper border around this ceiling
like the flowers in my mother's room
in the Memory Unit.
My husband's father died in this ER,
and no one cried but me.
I am trying to float free.

Have you had cancer?
No.
Have you had cancer?
No, but my father did.
I slept on the floor
of his hospital room
heard the machine suck
fluid from his stomach, touched
the urine bag in the dark. Hoped
it was warm. Wished
it was cold as ice.

My husband, curled
in the chair in the corner, asks,
"Are you all right?"
I think so.
"Are you all right"
Read the green numbers. Look at the numbers.
All I know for sure is if I look toward you,
tears slide to my bare chest.
I would rather look at the circling
flowers near the ceiling
or the needle in my vein.

Some Days

     I wish I had a wife
so I could lock myself in and write
while she tends to children and laundry,
prepares my food, and rubs my shoulders,
weary from working at this computer.

But I am the wife.
I know the geometry of the pantry,
warm sheets folded and held to my breast,
the sweet smell of basil
planted by my own hand.

I remember the yellow pot I bought
when the marriage changed,
the one that held ivy tied to a wire heart.
I clipped the leaves that tried to wander,
kept the painted pot and ivy heart in our bedroom.
Each week I cut back the wayward
heart-shaped leaves and let them fall.
He never noticed.

I Didn't Think of You

     didn't think of you at all today.
Then, as if you were
coming home tonight,
I thought of dinner.

Maybe two filets.
The corn you like is in season.
You might make a Caesar salad
the way you did
when the bowl was new,
and I loved watching
the drama of the dressing.

Or, I could pick up chicken breasts;
we could work together
over our wooden chopping block,
the one we bought at that auction
in Kalamazoo
and couldn't carry up the stairs.

We might stand
across from each other,
you chopping the onions
to spare me tears.

I could get finger food:
plump pink shrimp,
tiny stuffed tomatoes,
spicy redskin potatoes.

We could stretch out on the quilt
your grandmother made for us,
feed each other
in front of the fire.

For a while
driving home from work,
Darling,
I forgot you are gone.

The Day After a Lunar Eclipse

She wakes to birdsong.
Last night at 10:15,
she went alone to her window
and looked west with the wonder of childhood.
She remembered the light, the orange,
and the grapefruit in second grade
where her teacher, Miss Kettle, held
all the class in her embrace of enthusiasm.
Yellow shades covered the tall windows
of that classroom in Sibley School.
The only light shone from a flashlight
onto the fruit and reflected on Miss Kettle's face.
That night she could not find the moon
though she ran through the orchard,
the garden, and clover-filled lawn.
Last night she saw it, clear orange disc,
faint outlines of the face of the man, disappearing.
She remembered twelve years ago,
a beach house in Saint Marten.
She went to the window alone,
sad because her man slept.
She could hear him restless
in their bed. It was 2:30 AM.
That night she thought of packing
and leaving—finding that man
who would look in wonder
with her at lunar eclipses,
the first peony, the last leaf.

Today a cardinal is on the evergreen,
like flame on a green candle,
and she knows she can thrill
to the bird, its song, the candle
on this white canvas of snow alone,
alone with the same husband
still sleeping in her bed.

IV.

Cycles

Look, Mama, I'm Writing a Poem

I want to follow this line of words
back to the yellow kitchen
where round steak was pounded
with the chipped edge of a blue plate
and angel was the only cake
always made from egg whites
left over from the baby's breakfast
where sky-blue shells fell
from the nest in the maple
that was circled by a quilt
of crimson leaves each fall.

Mama, the sun is setting.
Lake Michigan is answering.
It is the pink time now,
the time of reflection.

I Am Always Forgetting Something

My car keys,
my best friend's name
in third grade,
my list of things to do,

my recipe for paprikash chicken,
how many are coming for dinner.
I forget and again
set an extra place.

I forget to water
the morning glories,
pull the thistles from the lilies,
deadhead the peonies.

I forget my lipstick color,
how to make fudge,
his blue eyes.

I wonder what happened to
my wedding shoes,
the penny for good luck,
his laughter.

It may all be buried with
the lists, the car keys,
the thistles, my recipes,
the wilted peonies.

Alzheimer's Unit: Room #653

She's dressed but asleep in bed,
her white hair a halo.
Cyclamen blossoms like butterflies
hover on her bedside table,
family looks on from frames.
Above her bed, a metal plaque,
Volunteer of the Year—Butterworth Hospital,
"Most Lifetime Hours of Any Volunteer."
I pick a browned cyclamen,
pluck out the mushy stem,
adjust the shade, bring more water.
"Who are you, my dear?"
"I am Linda."
"No, No! Linda is in school.
I packed her lunch this morning,
peanut butter and whole wheat,
cut into butterfly shapes,
orange sections like smiles
and a note, 'Mother loves you.'"
"Oh," I say and step closer.
"She's kind of bookie, too smart, you know.
I'm afraid she'll be on "old maid"
like her Aunt Cecilia."
"Mama, you have four grandchildren
and two great-grandchildren.
Look at them here in these pictures."
"No, Girl. Linda will be home for lunch soon.
We'll have strawberry ice cream for dessert
and watch *Guiding Light*
before she goes back to school."

I pull her pink volunteer smock from the closet,
the one covered in blue award pins.
"Mom, do you remember this? Mom?"
"Who are you? Get out.
Get my daughter Linda. Find my Linda."

She Forgets My Name Again

"Yes, Daddy was good
and brought us all candy,
but he loved you best.
You, Mother, in your flower-laden hats
were the prettiest mother at Sibley School.
No, your brain is fine. It's perfect.
You are healthy.
I am Linda. Remember?
Mom, I am not Lilac or Lily.
I am Linda.
Look in this album.
See my children, your grandchildren?
O, I was confused. The youngest is you.
This is your family. The woman I thought
was my daughter, Amy, is really
Annie, your Mother. Yes,
you are the baby in this book."
I remember Annie, pig hocks and sauerkraut,
bushels of potatoes we'd peel together.
Annie left a tag of peel on one
so we'd know which was mine.
O, Annie, what is mine now?
I am your bread bowl,
your century plant, the one that bloomed
for my fifth birthday.
I am the hollyhocks in your yard
and the daffodils and lilacs, even the lilies.
I am your granddaughter. I remember you.
Lenore, your youngest, was ninety last week.

She calls for you, Annie.
She says, "Mama, I need you."
Annie, please take her home.
I can let her go now.
She doesn't know my name,
but she remembers you.

Premature Pulling at the Botanical Gardens

Acres of purple mums flourished.
Like reckless dancers they surrendered
to the rhythms of waves of wind,
charming in the way only truth,
innocent of its beauty, can be.

Then came the premature pulling
for perfection's sake. A musty
layer of mulch covers the earth
where the lavender ladies
could have completed their dance,
returned to the soil. Become eternal.

First Snow

I walk into my study, and the world is changed:
a life-dividing moment like your first breath,
first step, first time you rode a two-wheeler alone,
like your first kiss, the time you left home
suitcase in hand and climbed the steps alone,
your first job, the day you decided to live together,
the birth of your child, her leaving for kindergarten
and not looking back, like the day you realized
your marriage was flawed just like your parents',
knew it was not to be a fairy tale,
like the death of your father,
and you were alone.

This morning I walk into this room,
see the first snow like a quilt on the yard,
deadheads of daisies, rabbit tracks like script—
a message—on the virginal snow,
skeletons of trees scrape the sky,
a few flakes still fall,
and I wondered how many more first
snows wait in line for me.

Widow In Spring

for Susan

Robins have returned.
She sees a familiar pair
feed each other,
gather grass and twigs,
begin their nest.

She goes to her shed,
finds forgotten bulbs in a wooden box.
The burlap bag says, *Plant in October
before the first frost.*

Without earth, water, or light,
these shriveled bulbs have pierced
their winter shrouds.

Last fall she took a single hyacinth bulb
and suspended it in a crystal vase.
Two intertwined blossoms grew.

She took the blooms to her husband.
Apples hung in the orchard. One
by one they all let go.

Now apple blossoms are bursting
on gray branches. She cradles
the bag of sprouting bulbs
to her breasts.

Bouquet

She goes to her garden at dawn
after a long twisted night.
The mourning doves are calling.

She gathers white bridal wreath
and pungent purple chive blossoms,
the first flowers of spring.

There are only two stalks left
on the bleeding heart bush.
She picks one with a few hearts hanging.

Pink rose petals brush
her bare legs as she goes
to the lilacs her husband planted.

When the flowers were lush,
she gathered armloads
and filled her empty spaces.

She searches the fading blossoms
and finds one fragrant flower.
The rest are brown-edged and dying.

The mourning doves are calling.

Cycles

Out my window, near
the wrinkled adobe wall,
bougainvillea bows
to the sun.
Fuchsia leaves
masquerade as flowers.
Call the bees.
Ask for sex,
which is a flower's
only destiny.
We think the beauty
is for us, a symbol
of something,
but it's really
all stamens, pistils,
and ovaries,
like a slim-hipped
girl brushing
her beauty.

Psychotherapist's Waiting Room

I.
Artificial noise
eight chairs
seven empty.

II.
Her sister sang at church,
sang all the way home
in the wagon.
They said, "She was dead
in the morning."
Her mother set
an extra place
at the dinner table
every night.

III.
This girl careened around
her block. She pumped
her own red wagon
with one leg pulled under her.
Bears lived in cages over the hill,
fat black bears that could cool
in their concrete pool.
After she watched the swimming bears,
a man took this girl to the woods
to show her more than baby flying squirrels.

IV.
There are eight empty chairs
in the waiting room.

Be Fruitful and Multiply

Bees sting.
Mosquitoes swarm.
She left her bed
to wander alone.

She wants to bite,
                          kick,
     scratch,
                                      scream,

chew up the cherry,
spit out the stone,
bite the damn apple,
let the juices flow.
Well, she wants to divide
like an overgrown rose.
She plans to grow thorns
where the wasted blood flows.

Timing

Does the bikini-clad girl
covered in pink patches
connected by gold chains
know?

In the time it takes
to turn over
to reapply oil
to unlined skin,

she will
be us.

Observing from under
a red umbrella
remembering when her
own power pulsed.

We, too,
thought
it would always.
be so.

Spider Plant

I hold my babies on strings,
feed them through
life-giving cords.
They grow roots
that reach out
into empty air.

Can any of us
survive
a severing?
Do I want
disconnection?
They are heavy, but
they repeat me,
even applaud me

on

long

thin

umbilical

cords.

V.

I Reclaim

Language

Two empty soda bottles in hand,
a girl taps the edge of the counter.
Her mother responds.
Rhythms repeated and reorganized.

The language of drums
like the baby in her chair
repeating *ball, bottle, book*.
Sounds tossed, caught, and repeated.

It is why I write: I want you
to nod in understanding,
like her mother did when
she found the music of *Mama*.

Perfect Pruning Shears

I am the bright blue iris that blooms
by her back door. I am as precious
as the black tulip that is rooted in her heart.
Five paper-wrapped messages
wait on my stalk.
They will open sequentially
in this garden of symmetry,
scatter yellow truth again.

Every day she comes
with those gold scissors,
prunes away the less than pretty.
Daffodils withered and wasted,
naked tulip stalks,
peony blossoms that
have sagged to the soil.

In this garden of symmetry, security, sameness,
every flower must be
the picture on the seed packet.

We flowers think
she should throw away her shears.
Let us be!
Tall as the sunflower,
free as the one-eyed daisy,
Let us ramble like the rose.

She could climb the cherry tree
live in the shifting clouds of beginnings,
let hummingbirds nest in her hair,
be washed by rain till
the golden scissors
grow green.

Risk of Impalement

from Grand Cayman

Lemon and lime trees cut back hard
flattened and wired to white lattice,
a yellow-footed egret passes.
His head undulates.
His body follows like a wave,
like a snake.

She wants to tell you
of twenty-nine years of marriage,
but the green book in her lap
on living in the present moment, tells her
not to travel backward and forward.
So, she must be with her hands now.
One holds a yellow spiral notebook.
The other moves a pen left to right.

Hard green Adirondack chair,
a fishtail palm showers shadows on her page.
Distorted lemon and lime trees
carry one-inch thorns
close to their hearts—
No room for any bird to perch, sing, savor
the green and yellow
flesh of the crucified trees.

Letter to My Long-Term Husband

I want you to wait under our oak trees,
water my tomato plants, pick the last peony,
and miss me like Donald Hall misses Jane.

I want you to remember
this isn't the first time I have left you.
And, honey, remember the body
that carried your children,
the breasts that no one else has touched
in thirty some years,
my office with its piles of papers
never to be sorted in the way you think right,
my purple clematis brought from the old house,
my grandmother's thimble,
your mother's wedding ring in my drawer,
her ashes in the gold and green box on your closet shelf,
the children we almost had, our children,
my hair in the sink, on your brush, on your pillow,
the Christmas cactus that was my mother's.
O, visit my mother; she forgot my name Thursday.

Remember the room where we first made love,
the tangled sheets, the slant of sun,
my body young as yours—remember.

I want you to remember, because
if you block my sun again,
I will leave you with the ashes and oak trees.
This time I really will.

Before the Telephone Rang

    the secret appeared at her side
as the stars faded,
It almost slipped through
her bitten blue pen.

She is the last drop of moisture on the maple leaf.
She is the one snowflake that could return to the sky.
She is the baby her mother carried
and her own babies.
She is the woman who wants
to rock to the rhythm of tides, drums, a heart-
beat. Ride the moon's spiral of seasons.

She carries her coiled history
like the nautilus,
like the rings of the maple,
like rings abandoned in a wooden chest.
Her ring will
not be buried in a box—
as her father's was—
like her mother's will be.

She takes the heavy stone,
finds truth hard enough
to shatter it to stars.
Stars for her hair,
    for her eyes,
for her enlightenment.

Conversation: Alzheimer's Unit

after Mark Strand

Mother, why did you have me?
I wanted a daughter
with long eyelashes.
Mother, why did you have me?
You were born ten months
after Pearl Harbor. I wanted
to save your father from war.

Mother, why do you cry?
I cry for Lorraine who died,
the sister whose name I bear.
Mother, why do you cry?
I cry because I never wanted
to be anyone's mother.

Mother, how are you now?
I am floating. I am Lorraine, the virgin.
My eyelashes are longer than yours.
Mother, how are you now?
My belly aches. This place you put me in
never gives me enough food.

Who are you, Mother?
No one. I raised myself.
Who are you, Mother?
Your grandmother, Anna,
who left her wedding ring
to you and not to me.

Mother, why did you tell me not to be too smart?
Because no man would want you,
you would be an "old maid."
Mother, why did you tell me not to be too smart?
Because your father loved learning
and left me for you.
Mother, do you love me?
I love you, my pretty.
Mother, do you love me?
You were born in one unendurable pain.
I was torn apart.

Rain Washes

    the maple's hands,
muddies the soil
around the perennials
they planted last weekend.

Yesterday's yarrow has collapsed.
Yellow saucer heads tilt.
Yarrow's wild cousin, Queen Ann's Lace,
remains—a throne for the purple queen.

Fuchsia phlox bend
with the breeze,
petals touch the ground
but have not buckled.

Daisy reaches still for the sun,
the reflection of its all-knowing
yellow eye. Daisy always
ready to decide.

Saffron daylilies trumpet—
open, ready, reckless, wanting—
unaware this is the only day.

She walks
to the struggling perennials,
loosens her hair,
lifts her hands to the rain.

Birthday

There are flowers in this house,
the sensual dance of stargazer lilies,
mums, cosmos, and roses.
It was my birthday Monday,
and my husband brought me
flowers: a bouquet
and a single pink rose
nestled in baby's breath.

The rose's leaves turned brown and brittle.
I've re-cut the stem and refilled the vase,
but the rose's pink petals are locked,
beautiful in their way
like the damaged daughter
he gave me,
   forever   a bud.

France After the Affair

We see the crumbling tower of a castle
from our balcony in Beaucastel,
drive through vineyards
toward the Rhone. The road dwindles,
becomes a flowery field. He spreads
the new blue and yellow tablecloth.
We share a ceremony of goat cheese,
olive topinade, tomatoes, and fresh bread,
open a bottle of wine, lie back on our tablecloth.
Later there will be fresh figs and grapes
as barges float by our castle.

We bought that cloth in Avignon,
where yesterday the mime stood sturdy,
the carousel glittered,
and a woman danced the Fandango alone.
Children followed a magician
amazed by his trail of scarves
and the surprise of a dove.
He took me to the carousel,
and Avignon blurred
as I felt his familiar hand
help me onto the white horse.
All I ever wanted seemed to be there:
the good man, the white horse,
starlight, and the music of childhood.

People Are Disappearing in Michigan

written after reading two articles in The Grand Rapids Press

Julia, 44, brown hair, green eyes, never
came home last night.
The Red Cross is searching.
It's 25 degrees.
Trees are dressed in tinsel,
lights frame frosted windows.
Twenty miles away in Allegan,
Henry, father of four,
did not came home from work,
twenty-four years at Perrigo packing vitamins,
and never late.
His wife could put biscuits in the oven at 5:50
knowing he would be home at six.
People gather in candle vigils, search
the woods and apple orchards.
A black helicopter scans
Lake Michigan's frozen shoreline.
Julia's car was found in Grand Haven near the pier.
Henry's 2007 black GMC truck is missing.
I want to picture Henry and Julia on I-75
heading south to Florida or the Bahamas,
a bag of potato chips between them,
just opened Cokes cool in their greasy hands.

Tomato

Red, round, ripe,
full of the sun's heat
familiar in my hand
like a newborn's head

Little pumpkin
of pleasure
dressed in
six scalloped leaves

Leaves that held
the flower
that needed
the bees or a breeze

To start the seeds
in these
red ovaries.

Sometimes,
there is
so much sex
in my sink,

I need to
turn away
and quickly brown
the bulbous onions.

I Reclaim

I reclaim the orchard.
Tear down the houses.
Plant trees.
I reclaim buds, blossoms, and bees.
I reclaim milk in glass bottles
left in a tin box, frozen cream
that rose to the top
broke open the seal.
I reclaim the lid I slid
off popping corn
to delight my dog
who ate the evidence.
I reclaim my father's lap,
towers of blocks built
for the thrill of their crash,
being able to rebuild
over and over.
I reclaim myself from rows of wooden desks,
crayons I must not peel, arithmetic facts,
surplus apples, and the names on the blackboard
under *We do not talk in work period*.
I reclaim the live monarch
I had to impale and spray
with fixative for Miss Mason
whose wall of breasts fed no one.

I reclaim the girl who finally refused
to kill a frog for the biology teacher.
I reclaim that girl and the right
to rebuild any tower
over   and over again.

About the Author

Linda Leedy Schneider is an award winning poet, writing mentor, and psychotherapist in private practice. She has been a faculty member at Aquinas College and Kendall College of Art and Design. Her volunteer work in orphanages in Albania served as a catalyst for her writing and subsequent publications.

Linda is the recipient of a Readers' Choice Award from Pedestal magazine. She has been honored by the Dyer-Ives Poetry Competition and was nominated for a Pushcart Prize.

Linda reads her work frequently and has been featured at many venues including: The Saturn Poetry Series, NYC; The Back Fence, NYC; and Prairie Fire Poetry Series, NYC. She produced a reading for the international women's anthology, *Not A Muse* (Haven Books, 2009) at The Bowery Poetry Club, NYC.

Linda leads writing workshops nationally including a weeklong session annually for The International Women's Writing Guild of which she is a long time member. She is a strong mentor and has been able to support new writers in achieving their professional goals and publishing their work. She believes that a regular writing ritual leads to discovery, authenticity, personal growth, and even JOY.

www.ingramcontent.com/pod-product-compliance
Lightning Source LLC
Chambersburg PA
CBHW052106070526
44584CB00017B/2357